This book belongs to a little Bambou :

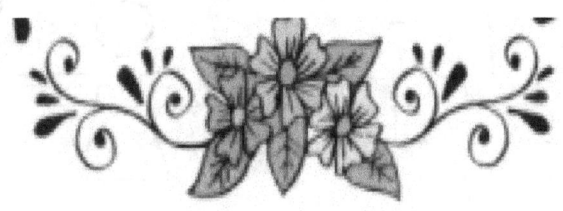

Numbers

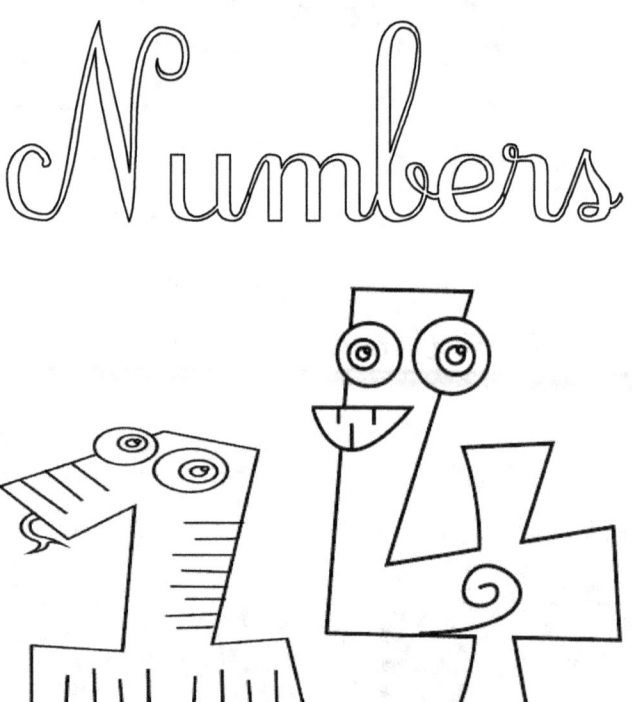

1

One

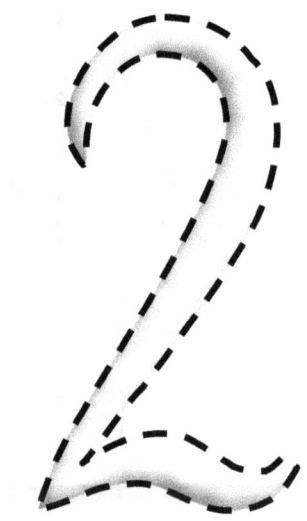

Two

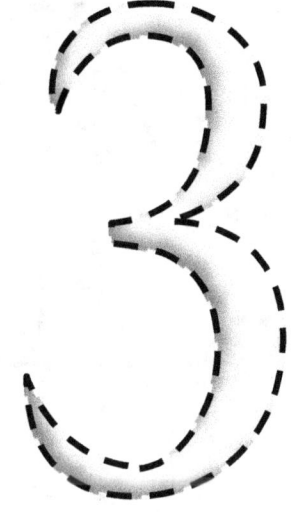

Three

4

Four

5

Five

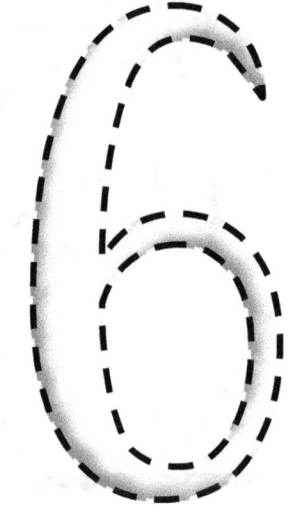

Six

7

Seven

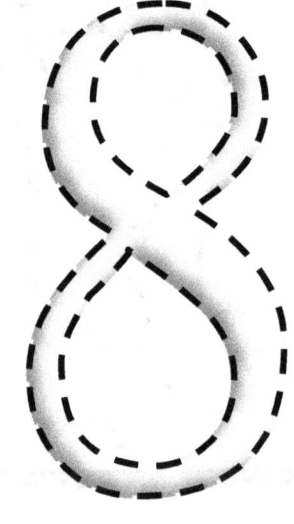

Eight

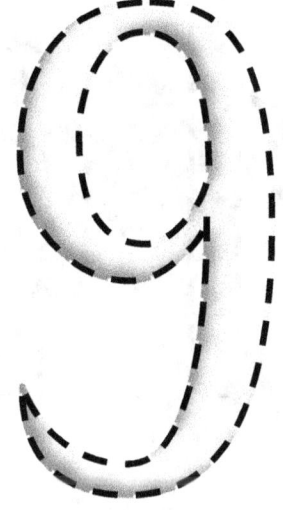

Nine

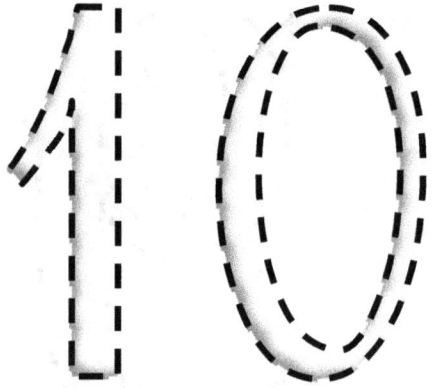

Ten

Number of rectangles

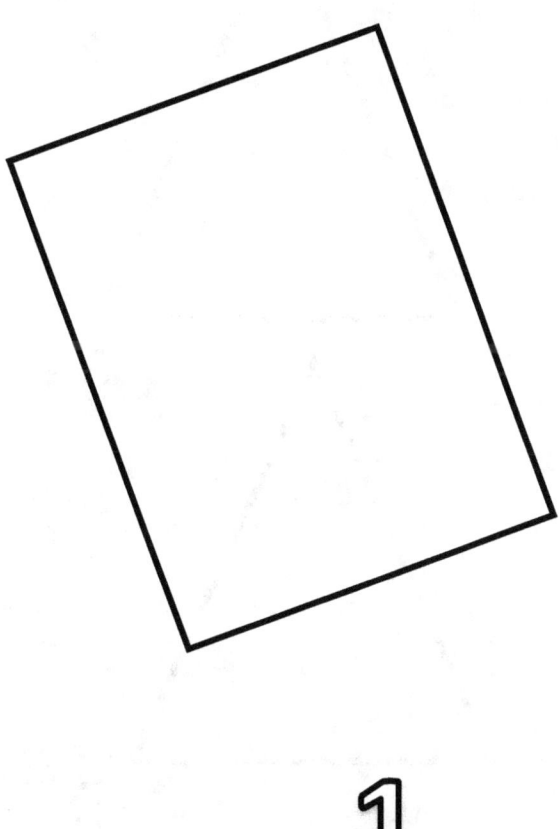

1

Number of triangles

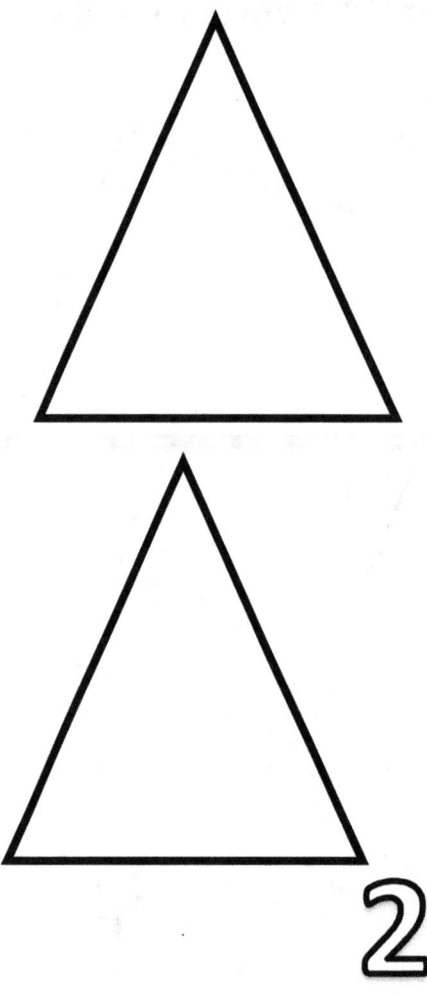

2

Number of circles

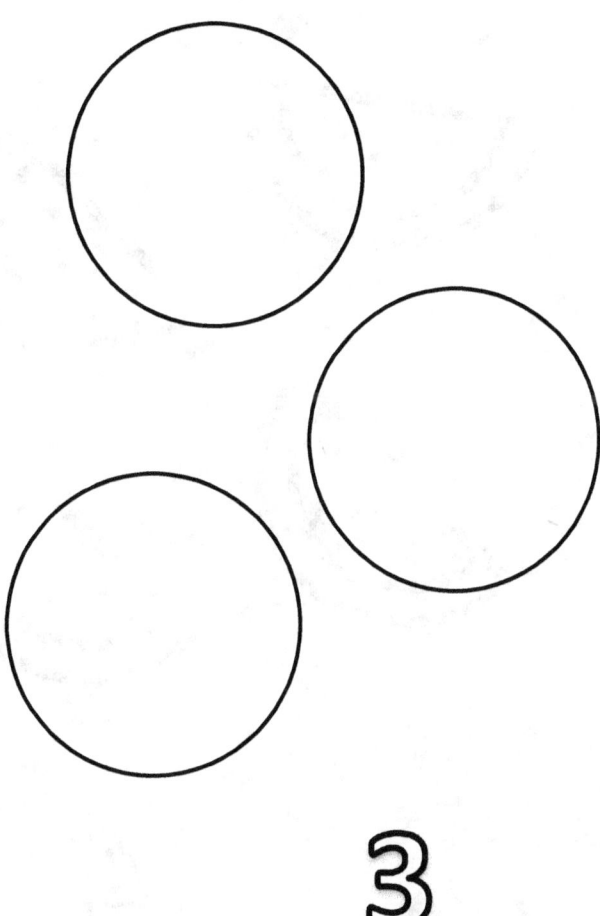

3

Number of watermelon

Number of grapes

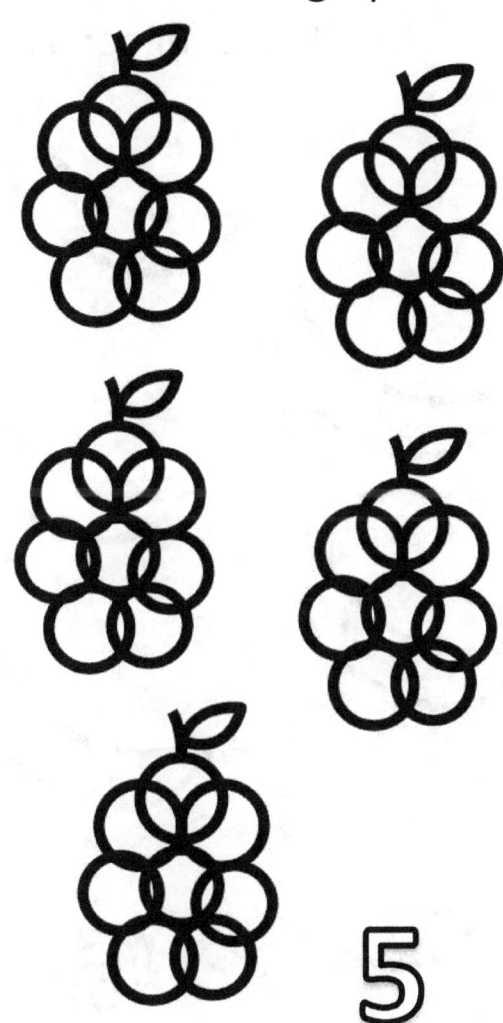

5

Number of bananas

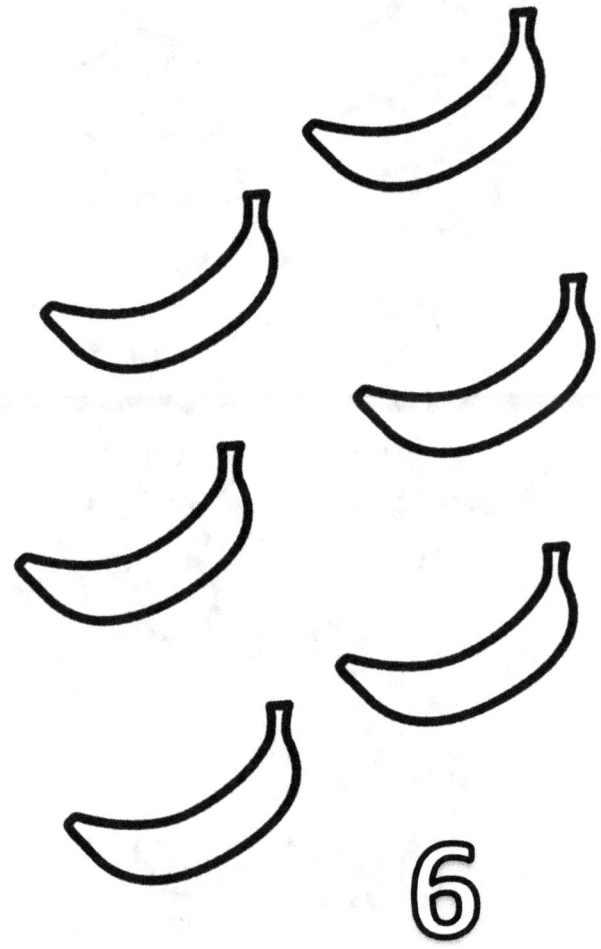

6

Number of oranges

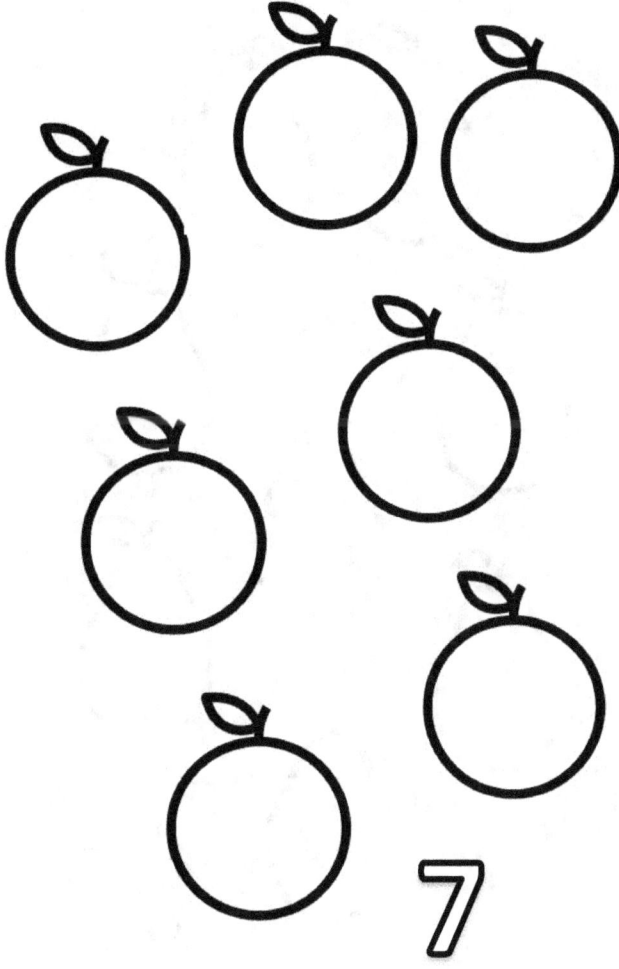

Number of pears

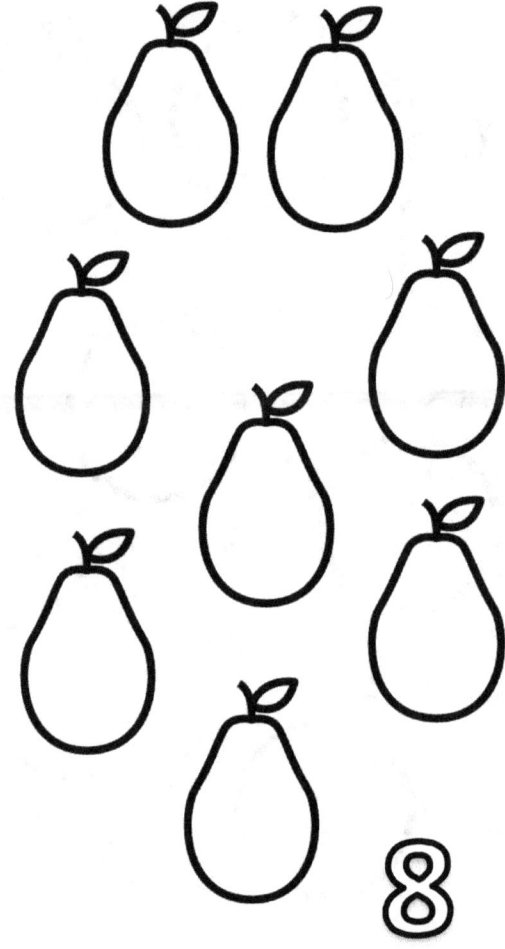

Number of strawberries

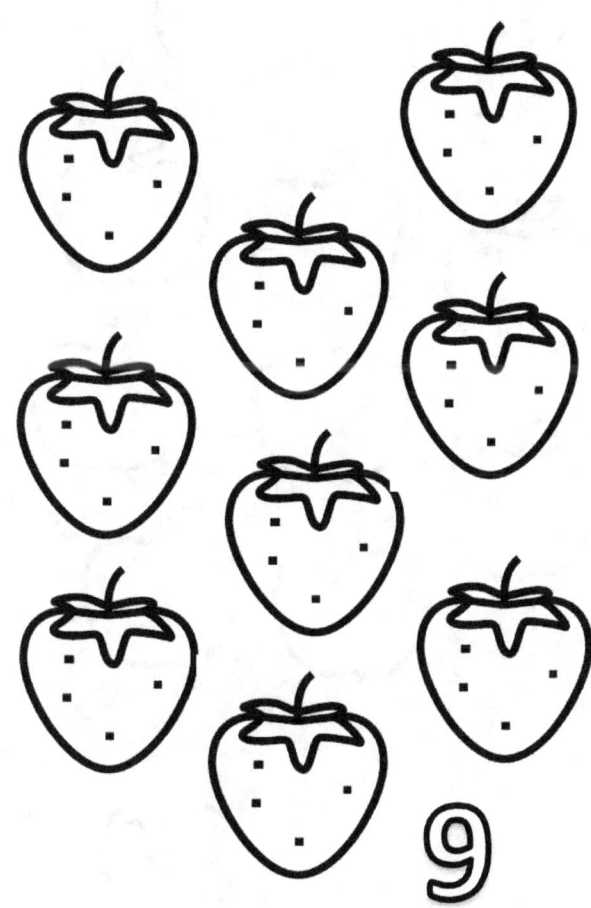

Number of apples

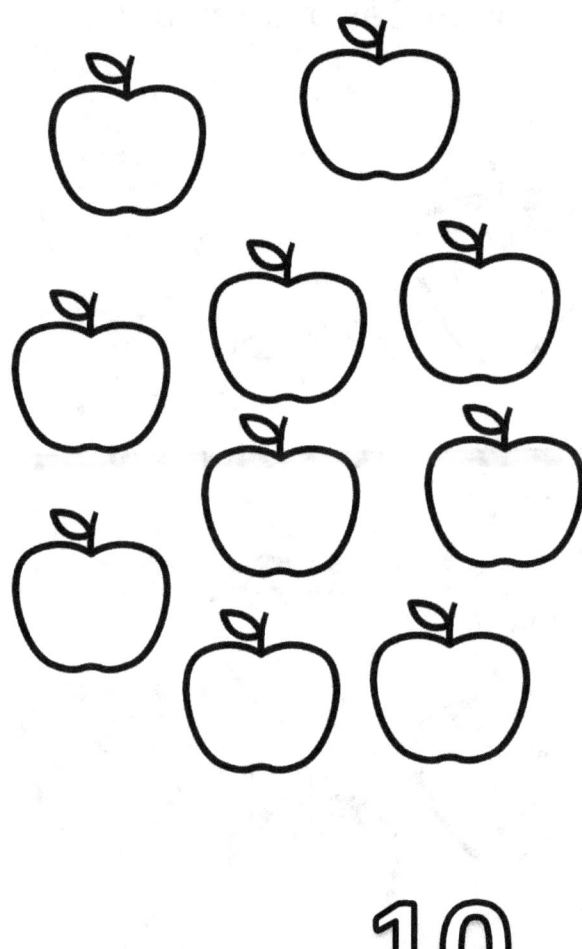

10

Alphabet

M T

A a

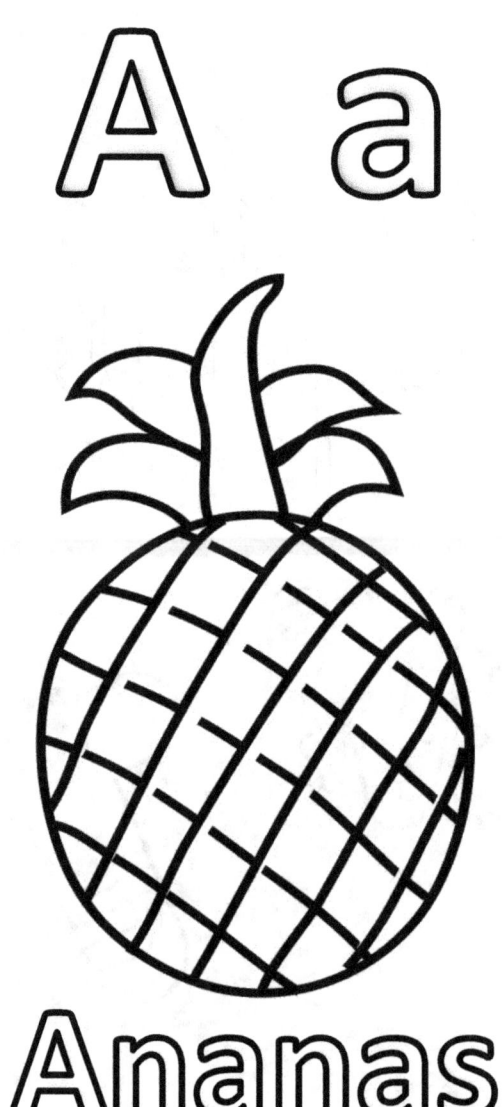

Ananas

A *A* *A*

a *a* *a*

B b

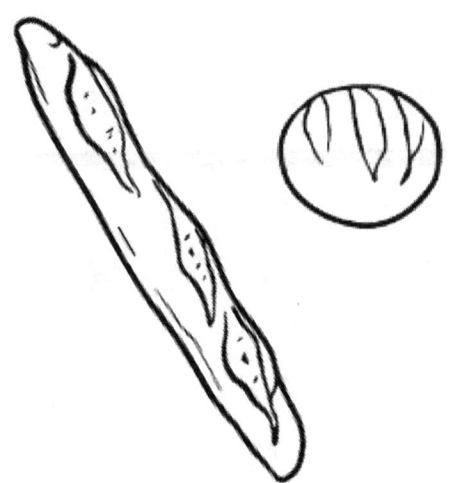

Bread

$\mathcal{B}$ $\mathcal{B}$ $\mathcal{B}$

ℓ ℓ ℓ

C c

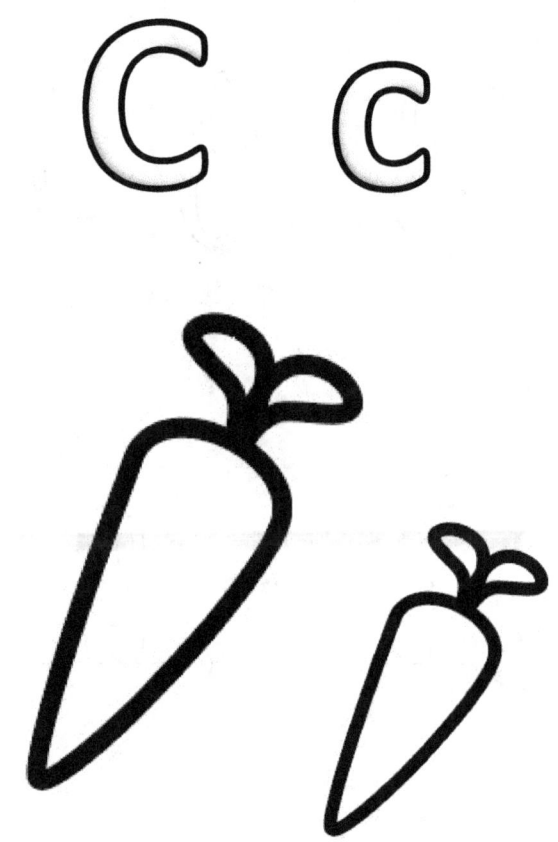

Carot

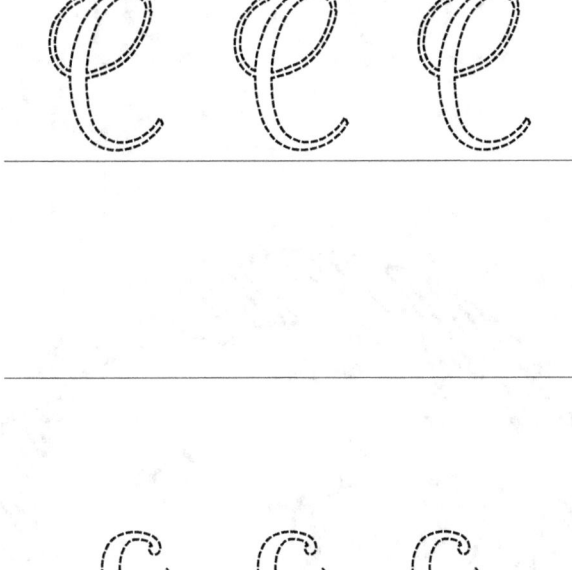

D d

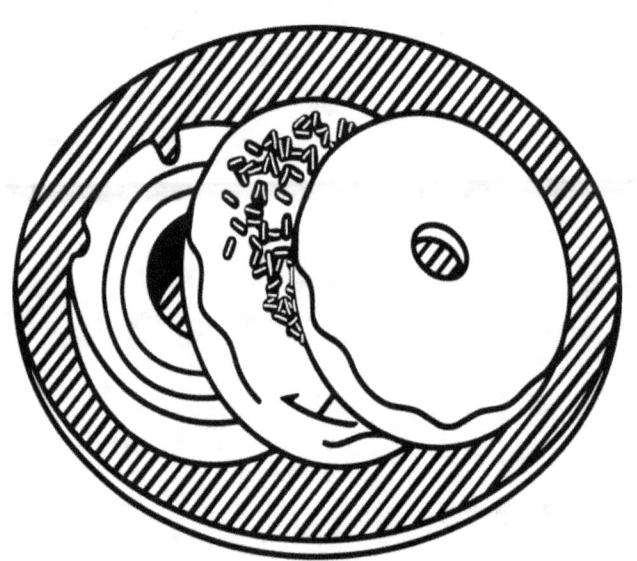

Donuts

$\mathcal{D}$ $\mathcal{D}$ $\mathcal{D}$

d d d

E e

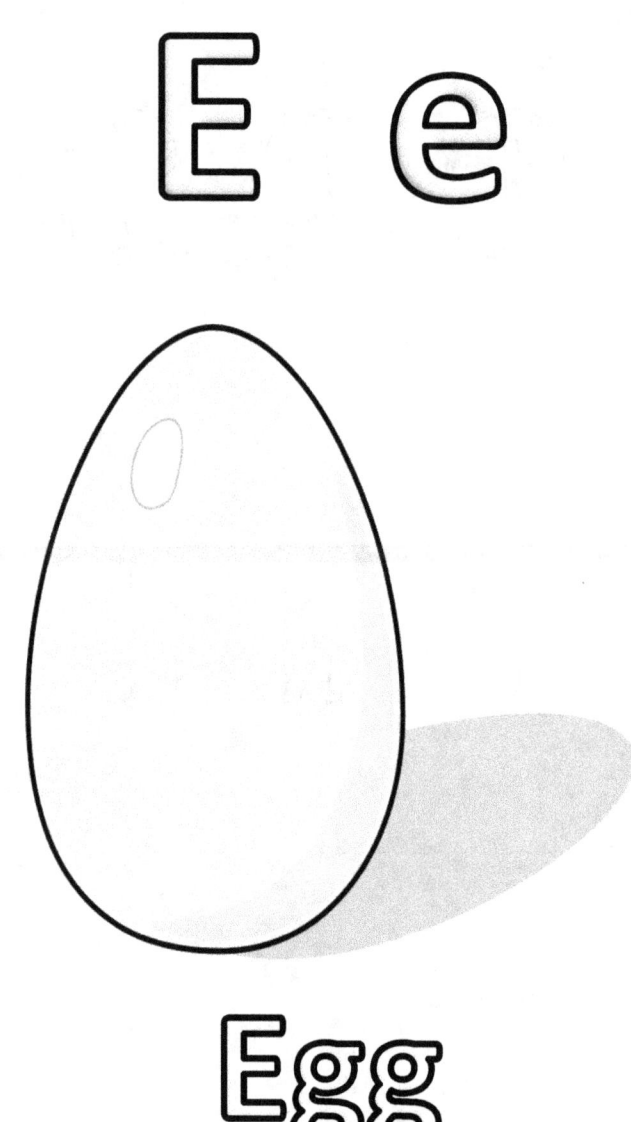

Egg

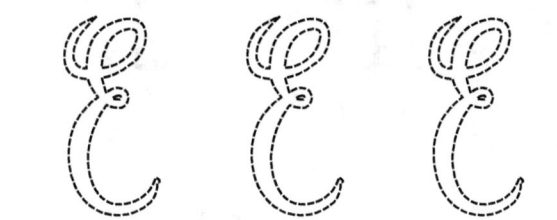

F f

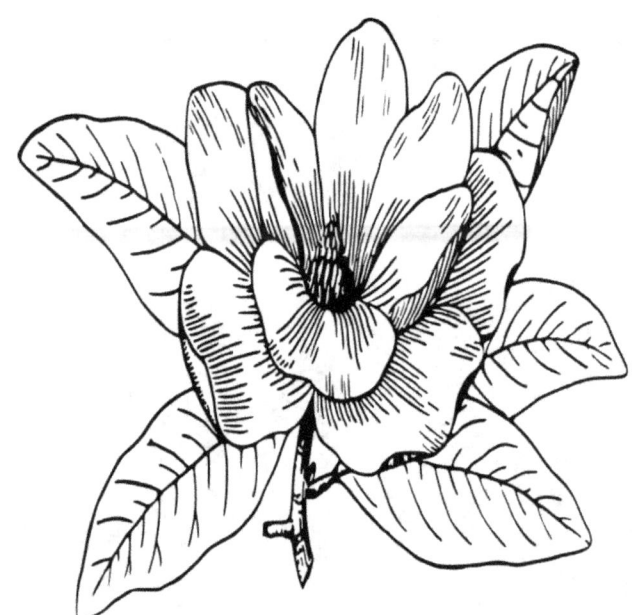

Flower

$\mathcal{F}$ $\mathcal{F}$ $\mathcal{F}$

f f f

G g

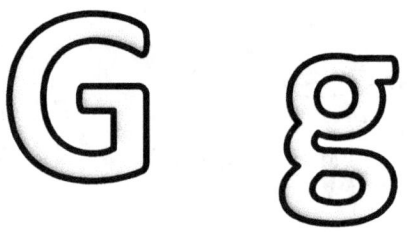

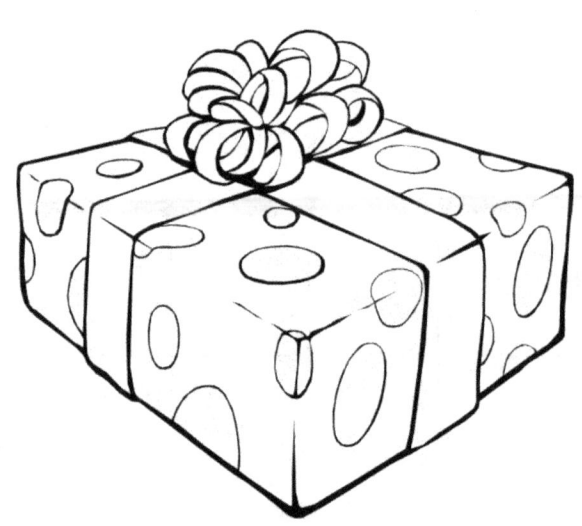

Gift

g g g

g g g

H h

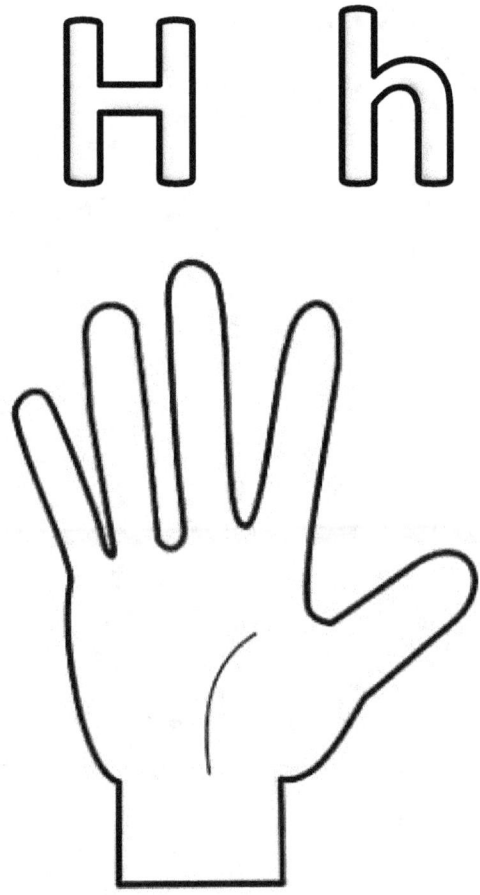

Hand

$\mathcal{H}$ $\mathcal{H}$ $\mathcal{H}$

h h h

I i

Ice cream

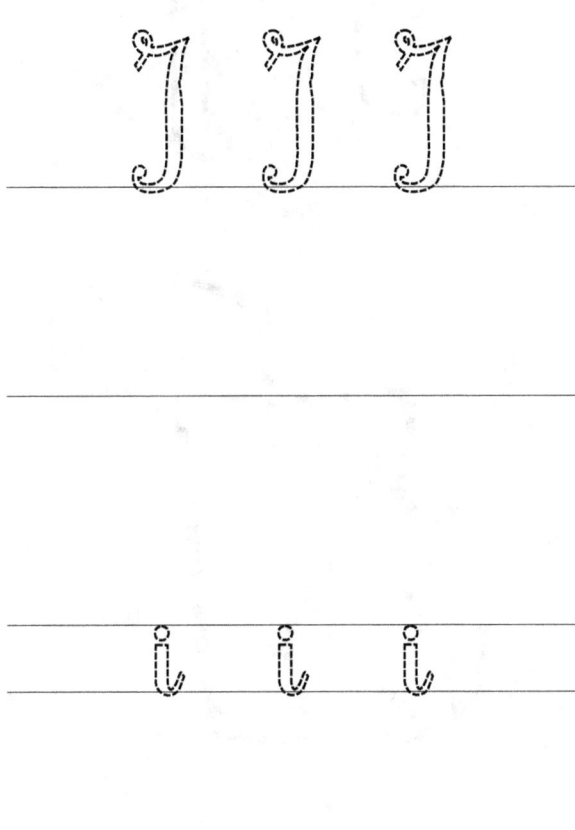

J j

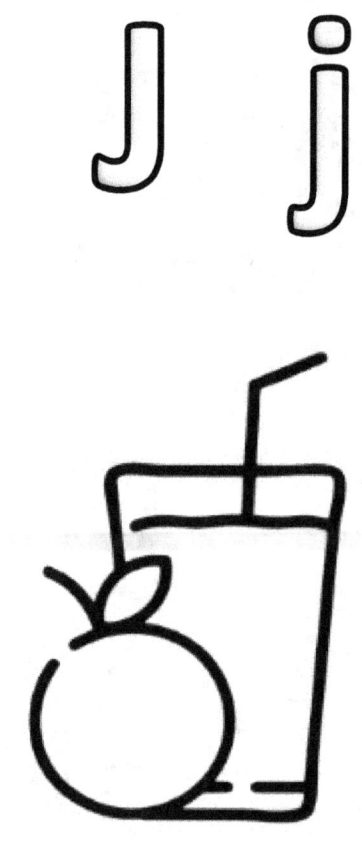

Juice

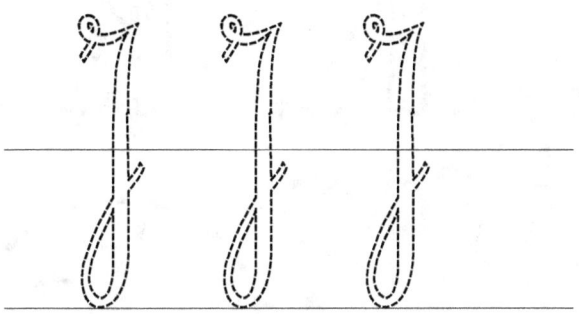

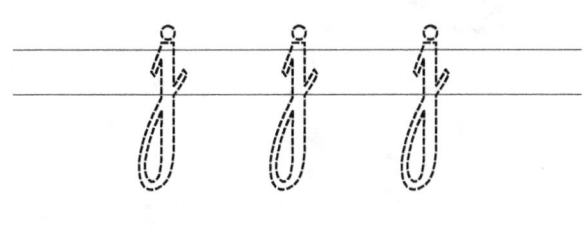

K k

Key

$\mathcal{K}$ $\mathcal{K}$ $\mathcal{K}$

k k k

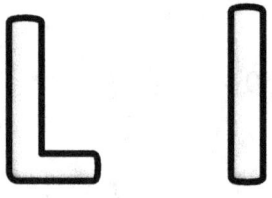

L l

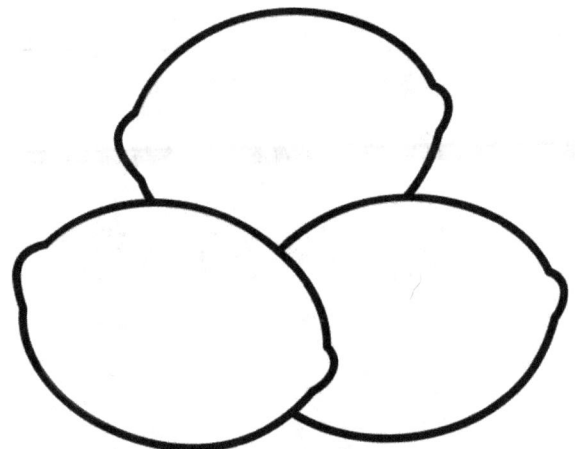

Lemons

$\mathcal{L}$ $\quad$ $\mathcal{L}$ $\quad$ $\mathcal{L}$

l $\quad$ l $\quad$ l

M m

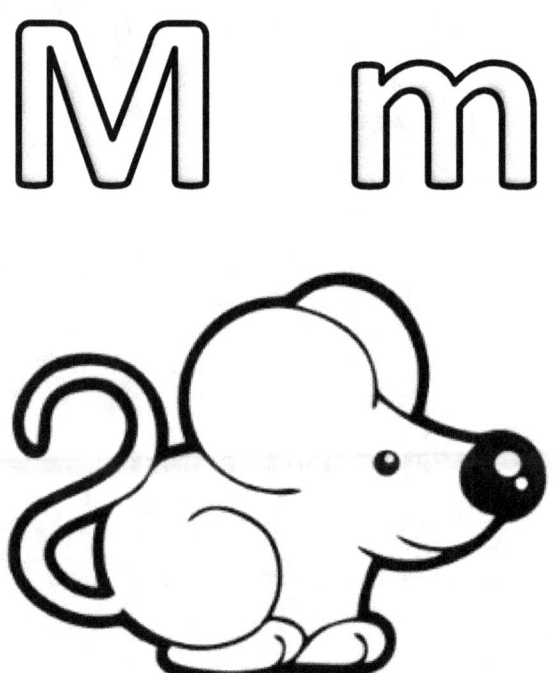

Mouse

M *M* *M*

m *m* *m*

N n

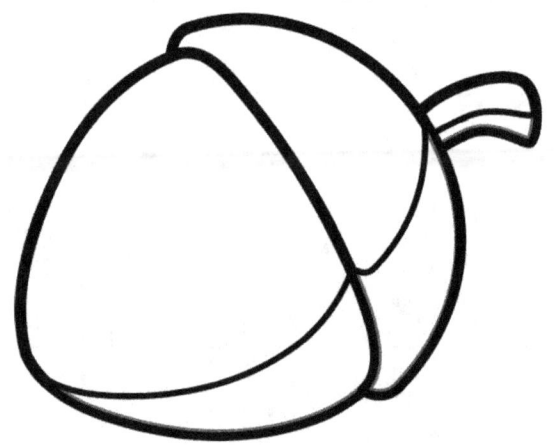

Nut

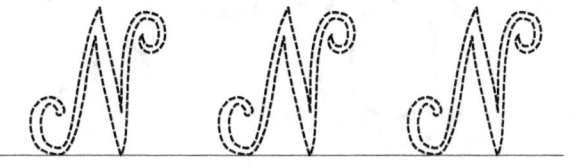

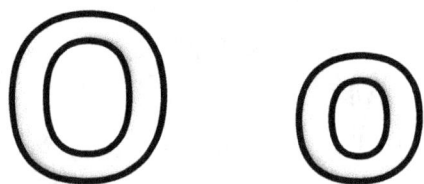

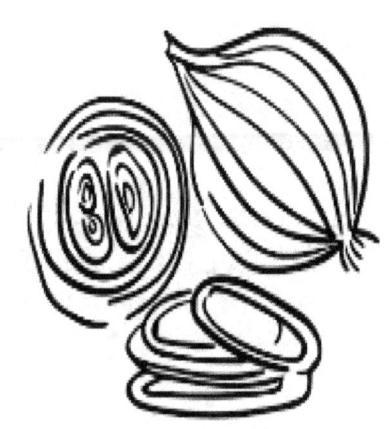

Onion

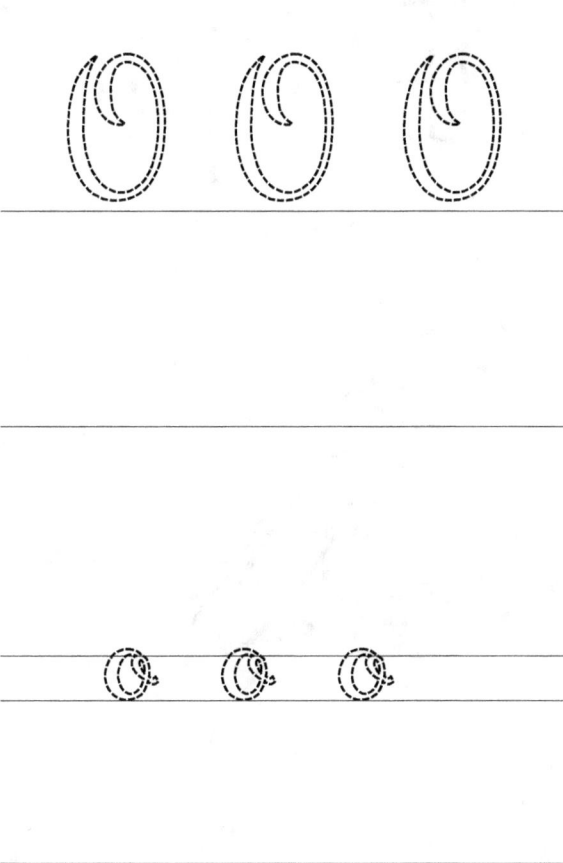

P p

Pencil

$\mathscr{P}$ $\mathscr{P}$ $\mathscr{P}$

r r r

Q q

?

Question

q q q

q q q

R r

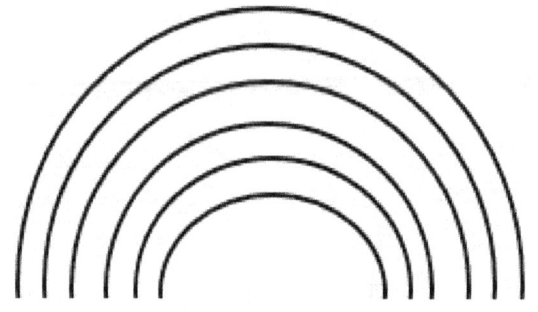

Rainbow

R *R* *R*

n *n* *n*

S s

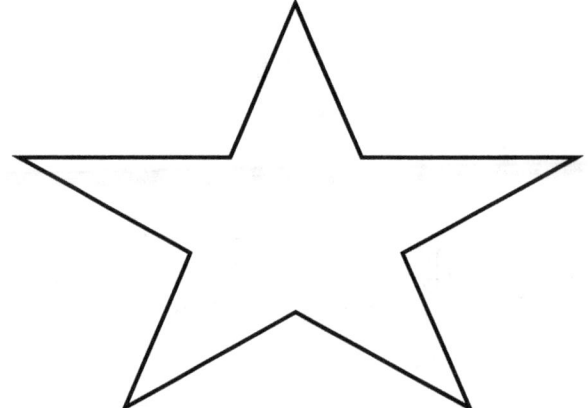

Star

S *S* *S*

T t

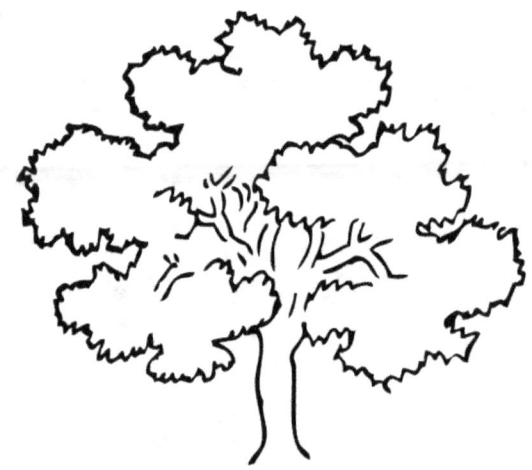

Tree

𝒳 𝒳 𝒳

t t t

U u

Umbrella

Ա Ա Ա

ա ա ա

V v

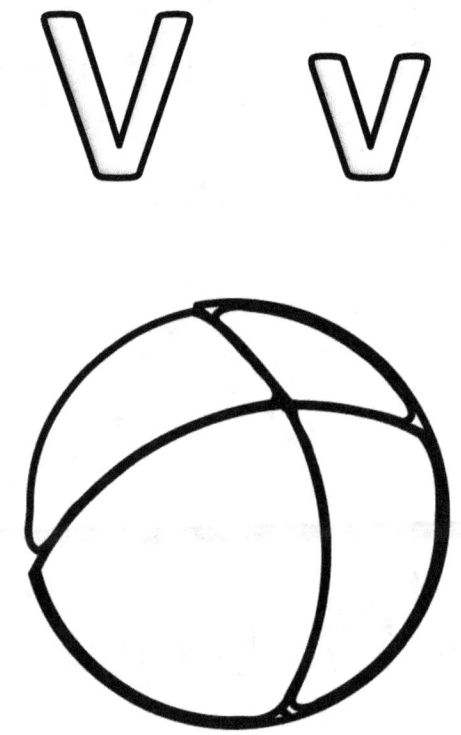

Volley Ball

𝓥 𝓥 𝓥

𝓋 𝓋 𝓋

W w

Water

$\mathcal{W}$ $\mathcal{W}$ $\mathcal{W}$

w w w

X x

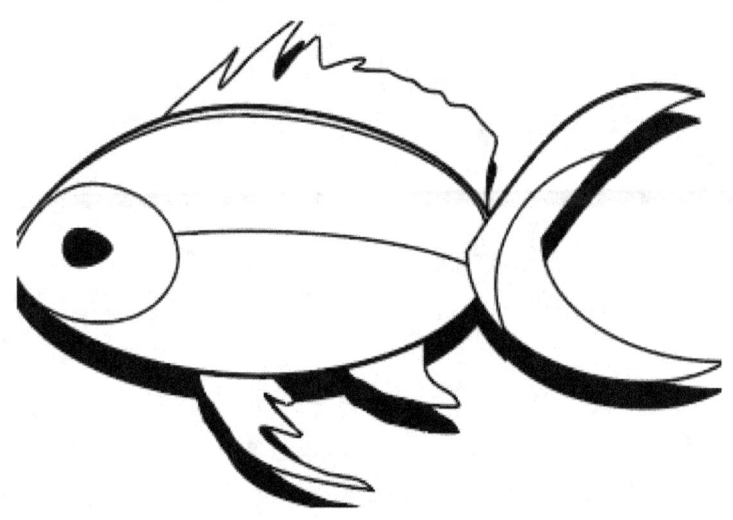

Xray fish

ℋℋℋ

𝓸𝓬 𝓸𝓬 𝓸𝓬

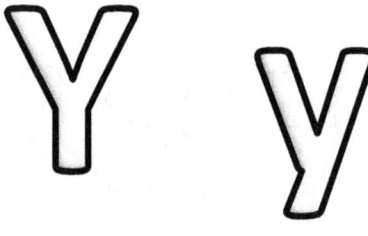

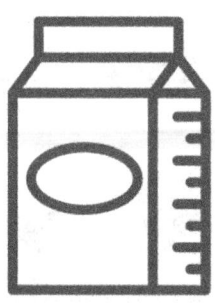

Yoghurt

y y y

y y y

Z z

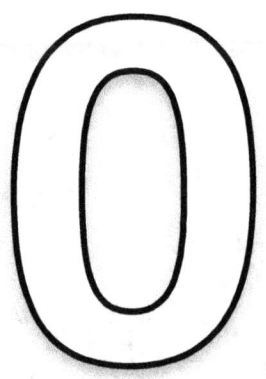

Zero

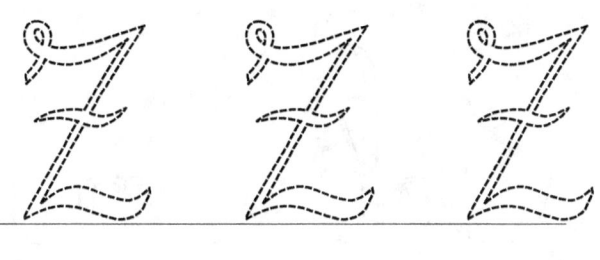

Coloring section

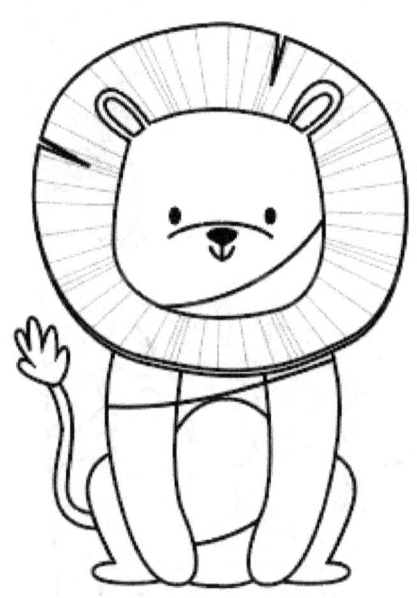

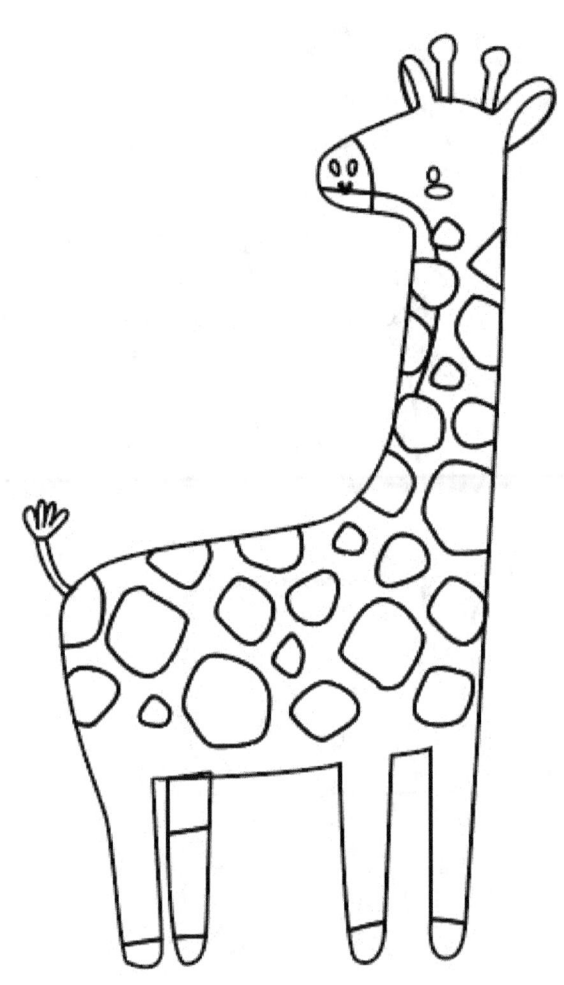

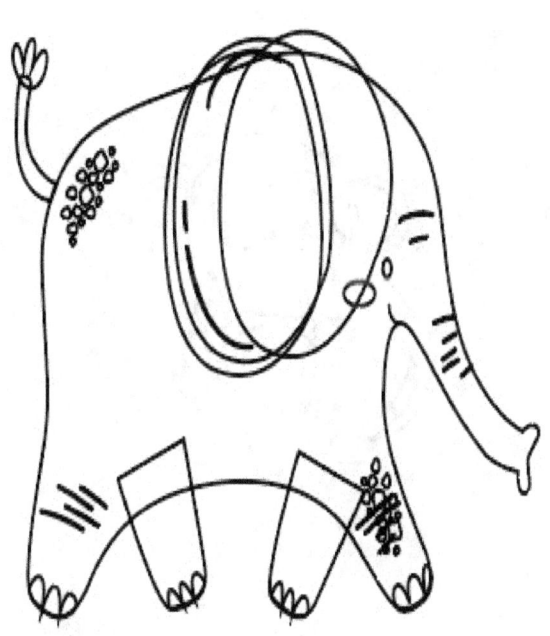

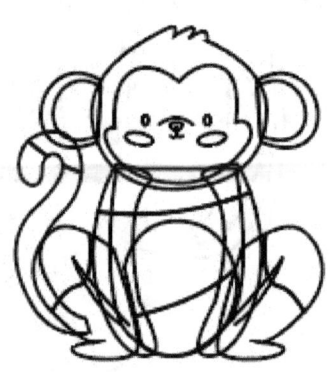